"Catawall!"

by
Te Harrison - Best

Copyright©2012 Te Harrison-Best

The right of Te Harrison-Best to be identified as the author of the work has been asserted by her in accordance with the Copyright, Designs and Patents Act 1988.

Design by Kookie Birjukov

ISBN 978-1-84986-022-2

This digitally printed version is 2012, is published in association with "Cuttlefish Publishing Ltd"

By

OTCEditions

An imprint of

ORION TRADING COMPANY UK LTD
Registered under the Companies House Act
Number 4968193

Website: www.otceditions.co.uk

This book is in copyright. Sold subject to the conditions that it shall not by way of trade or otherwise, be lent, hired out or resold or otherwise circulated in any form of binding without the written permission of the publisher.

A catalogue record for this book is available from the British Library

Acknowledgements

A huge thanks to everyone who has had a hand in turning this book into a reality.

Firstly, Stuart, my husband, who gave me such help, encouragement and support at every stage. Then, in no particular order, Lorraine Stack, her support has been inspirational; Rachel Chard, thanks for the additional pair of eyes; Linda Arthur, for her judgment and support; our three children, who just believed; Kookie for layout, design and enthusiasm; our five (now sadly three) cats and finally various other people's cats, and their staff!

And finally the cats everywhere that don't have the luxury of staff.

It is the intention of both the author, Te Harrison-Best, and Cuttlefish Publishing that a percentage of the profits from Catawall will be donated to cat based charitable organisations. For details of donations as they are made and the organisations that they are made to, please visit our web site www.catawall.com.

Our preferred charity and the one that will be receiving the 'lions share' of any donations is 'The London Persian Cat Rescue Centre'.

The London Persian Cat Rescue Centre

"We have been operating, in one form or another, for over 20 years, re-homing both Persian and other pedigree cat breeds. We work collaboratively with both the mainstream animal rescue organisations and other Pedigree Breed Welfare Groups. We also work with other Persian rescue groups outside of London.
For more details of us and our work, please see our website www.london-persian-rescue.co.uk."

London Persian Cat Rescue is pleased and delighted to be chosen and wishes 'Catawall' every success!

Dedication

This book is dedicated to our three grandchildren, Joshua,
Finlay and Eleanor, they allow me to stay in touch with the child within.
And Lola, a fellow cat lover and dear friend.

The Pill

You'd think it would be easy
to medicate a cat.
He seems so sweet and furry
or is that really fact?

He appears to spot a tablet
from twenty feet away.
A skirmish has commenced now,
a state of real melee.

You sidled up beside him
to administer the pill.
This has become a duelling clash
with man and cat at will.

You have a fleeing cat now,
the chase has just begun.
You grab him in a bath towel
but still he tries to run.

He's swaddled, and now hissing,
and the pill has hit your face.
You plonk it back into his mouth
with little style or grace.

He's stopped with all his antics,
the struggle is no more.
The cat is walking off outside
whilst the pill is on the floor.

Curtains

Oops I've gone and done it now,
my people will go spare
I've ripped their brand new curtains,
there's now a gaping tear.

I didn't know they were best silk,
imported from afar.
I had a little climb in mind,
but not to go that far.

Perhaps I could conceal it,
or blame it on the dog.
There is a risk they'll smell a rat,
or spot a guilty mog.

I really think I've cooked my goose
and things are looking bad.
Maybe they'll forgive this puss,
the one that's looking sad.

Maybe I should limp round
to feign an injured paw.
Or lay down looking rather ill
upon the kitchen floor.

I think I'd better pack my things,
and look for pastures new,
or make myself extremely scarce
before the air turns blue.

Mrs O'Donnell and her Black Cat Jack

Mrs O'Donnell's black cat Jack
has only three legs and walks with a clack.
She adores old Jack despite his flaws,
regardless of his fewer paws.

Jack, her boy, is a faithful chap.
He purrs like a rocket as he sits on her lap.
They both survive on pilchards for tea
and take little toddles along to the sea.

Mrs O'Donnell, she walks with a stick
and three legged Jack just isn't too quick.
Stopping halfway to take in some air,
it's a daily traipse for this odd little pair.

Upon their return they sit and watch telly
and Mrs O'Donnell tickles Jack's belly.
It's always milk and crackers before they retire.
It's the usual routine as they sit by the fire.

Old Mrs O'Donnell goes off to bed,
Jack wobbles behind her minus his leg
Jack nestles beside her then snores like a drain,
but Mrs O'Donnell would never complain.

A Venting Vet

Will you please control your crazy cat,
he's causing such a stir.
He's stampeding around the waiting room,
and nothing will deter.

He came here for his yearly check
and a booster in his rear.
He saw the hypodermic spike
and hollered out in fear.

We chased him up the curtain pole
and yanked him by the tail.
He shot across the treatment room,
to stop him we did fail.

We tried to call and coax him back.
He hissed and spat some more.
Then Nurse Malone did wrestle him
on to the lino floor.

Lucifer is waiting here
entwined with Nurse Malone.
So hurry back to claim your cat
and take him to his home.

Dinner Guest

Look who's come to dinner,
it's that cat from number four.
He's wafted through our cat flap,
that's in the garden door.

He's noshing on our food right now,
just like a refugee.
It's not that we're complaining much,
but he's already had his tea.

He seems a constant visitor
and we don't want him here.
We want you to send him off
with a flea that's in his ear.

His appetite's voracious
and he's getting really big.
He's starting to resemble
a Gloucester Old Spot pig.

We need a sound solution
to stop him from his feast,
So we can eat our cat food,
and leave us all in peace.

Tiger the Terrible

My cat looks ferocious,
with great big pointed fangs.
He's braver than the biggest lion
or the super hero gangs.

Nobody messes with Tiger
as he's bigger than a bear.
Other cats will flee from him,
he only has to stare.

Even dogs avoid him,
they shake in total fear.
You hear their four knees knocking
whenever he comes near.

The postman's also frightened
and runs fast for the gate.
Tiger chases after him,
he wants to be his mate.

Mummy says he's terrible
and should be locked away,
but I think Tiger's wonderful
'cause he brightens up my day.

I think she really loves him
because she strokes him so.
She would never ever throw him out,
or tell him he must go.

I don't need silly teddy bears
to comfort me to sleep.
Just having Tiger on my bed,
my big, striped, furry, heap.

What's in a name?

My owner calls me Tiddles
and I think my name is daft.
I should be called Goliath, Zeus,
or maybe even Darth.

My ears are nicked and craggy,
my fur's quite tattered and torn.
My undercarriage is saggy
and drags across the lawn.

My name is so important
so Tiddles will not do.
I'm king of the urban jungle,
a killer through and through.

So this kittie's now protesting
to the court of feline rights.
A campaign that's worth investing,
for the 'under cats' real plight.

A Moggies Tale

Who wants the finest pedigree
when you're out just chasing mice ?
Or a name that sounds exotic
like some oriental spice ?

Who wants to be at cat shows
and stuck inside a crate ?
When running after sparrows
is really rather great.

Who wants to be all manicured
and dunked inside a bath?
When it would be so much nicer
just sprawled across the path.

Who wants to be a house cat,
if open space is there ?
Unless you've trapped a little mouse
behind the kitchen chair.

Who wants to be looked after
with luxuriant grandeur ?
I think I'll change my mind right now,
for this I could endure.

Beast of Bodmin

You know the Beast of Bodmin,
the one found on the moor.
It's really my cat Cyril,
he's the size of a big barn door.

I wouldn't overstate his size,
or tell a whopping lie,
but Cyril's really, really big.
In fact he's ten feet high.

His head's the size of a dustbin
and his paws are just like ski's.
His tail is like a whiplash
and he's the host of ten inch fleas.

You think I would exaggerate
or spin a yarn or two ?
Next time you call out Cyril
you'll see it's really true!

Magnificent Moggie

She prides her self as rather chic,
her coat all groomed and very sleek.
With claws that are kept sharp and neat,
her pedigree, for her, complete.

Her whiskers are precision clean,
they're shaped and manicured as seen.
Her tail stands both long and lean,
she is that magnificent moggy queen.

She would insist her meals are light
and never eats too late at night.
Her food must be a fresh delight,
no tins or packs for her, alright?

It should never come as a surprise
since she would never compromise.
She might just flash those golden eyes
or sink her claws into your thighs.

Her mood can switch within a wink
before you had some time to blink.
The swishing tail would never kink,
you better move quite fast, I think.

This stunning queen just tops the league,
a classy cat, we're all agreed.
The way she acts leaves us intrigued.
She is that perfect cat indeed.

Our Ginger Tom

Next time you hear a commotion
it maybe our old cat.
He maybe on a red-hot date,
or in pursuit of a juicy rat.

You wouldn't call him pretty,
in fact he looks a state.
With tufts of fur gone missing
and his tail's no longer straight.

His manners are disgusting,
he really doesn't care.
Napkins are for sissies,
not for ginger toms to wear.

Despite all Tom's short comings,
and his general lack of style,
he's one cat in a million
and stands out by a mile!

The Duvet Tale

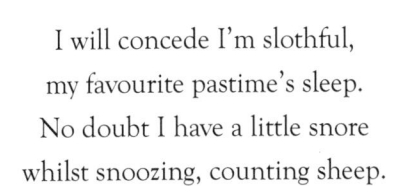

I will concede I'm slothful,
my favourite pastime's sleep.
No doubt I have a little snore
whilst snoozing, counting sheep.

Your duvet is inviting
to a cat who feels fatigued.
To nuzzle down so readily
must leave you quite intrigued.

My reputation for inertia
is renowned to say the least.
Sometimes I even stir myself
to have my nightly feast.

Eating is quite tiring
and exhausted cats should rest.
So I'm off to find the duvet now,
to do what cats do best.

Goodnight!!

Lazy

You can't really call me lazy,
I just need to rest my eyes.
In fact I'm really so alert,
so what you say are lies.

Who wakes you in the morning
at four thirty, without fail?
I even give your face a wash
before my morning wail.

What is it with you humans,
to complain because I sleep?
For me to keep my kitten looks,
it's a price that isn't cheap.

For when I'm on my rampage
and catch a bird or two,
you yell and scream obscenities
and then the air turns blue.

Next time I catch you napping,
in your favorite fireside chair,
I will pounce upon your comfy lap
and I'll give you such a scare.

You'll wish I was bone idle
and slept my life away.
This battle's lost, I really think,
as I will win the day.

Catching Spiders

Catching spiders is such fun,
they love to run away.
Oh boy, they give me much delight,
as I give chase and play.

I love the fact they have eight legs,
which makes them go quite fast.
The game we play goes on and on,
for hours it can last.

I'm sure that spiders love this game,
but not as much as me,
as they run around in circles,
when their legs are down to three.

I hope that they come soon again,
as my people are so thrilled,
since nothing gives them pleasure more,
than a spider I have killed.

Indignity

I caught my first bird today
and brought it home to mum.
She screamed and screamed and screamed again,
and now my hearing's numb!

She threw me out the cat flap
and took the bird from me.
I yowled and yowled and yowled some more
in total harmony!

How dare she rob me of my bird
for that she'll pay most dearly.
Next time I'll bring a smelly rat.
She'll rue the day, quite clearly.

Alphabet from a Cat
Humans, please take note.

A is for aloofness, found in every breed.
B is for those battered ears, from skirmishes indeed.

C is for that catnip, which many cats adore.
D is for those dreaded dogs, a kink in Newton's law.

E is for such elegance, found in every cat.
F is for me falling flat, disproving that last fact.

G is for the gracious ways, awarded to the few.
H is for the horror, things smashed to Timbuktu.

I is for ingratitude, as their staff should serve them well.
J is for the jingle, of that awful collar bell.

K is for the kittenish airs, when things just tend to break.
L is for me lapping cream, from around that chocolate cake.

M is for meowing, demanding to be fed.
N is for me nipping toes, while you're fast asleep in bed.

O is for the opening tins, a sound cats find divine.
P is for tinned pilchards, a taste that's quite sublime.

Q is for the quite time, which is often many hours.
R is for the roll around, especially on the flowers.

S is for me sitting down, upon the ironing pile.
T is for transferring fur, for that there's no denial.

U is for unforgiving looks, when visiting the vet.
V is for the vengeance mine , a dish cold you won't forget.

W is for wailing loud in the middle of the night.
X is for the Xmas trees, a climbing frame delight.

Y is for a great big yawn, a rest when fun is done.
Z is for is for me catching zzzz's, relaxing in the sun.

So now you know my alphabet, those words from A to Z,
And if you want to know some more, you'll find me on your bed !

Your Lucky Day

Oh little mouse, I see you there
underneath that fireside chair.
Your glowing eyes are full of fear,
you shake and squirm as I grow near.

Just see this as your lucky day,
for I will let you get away.
As I have eaten well tonight,
your scrawny bones will be alright.

This advice I give, dear mouse,
you never enter again this house.
For if you find me not replete
you, dear mouse, I will surely eat.

Someone Rather Special

Fang, she was a tiny cat
with nerves as strong as steel.
How she stood her ground indeed,
a sight that was surreal.

A marvellous hunter through and through,
no rodent could escape.
With lightening speed she would appear,
that tiny feline shape.

But despite her little dainty size
her claws were sharp as pins.
The furniture would vouch for that
and all our human skins.

With amber eyes that flashed when cross,
complete with swishing tail,
it wasn't wise to cross this queen,
as you would only fail.

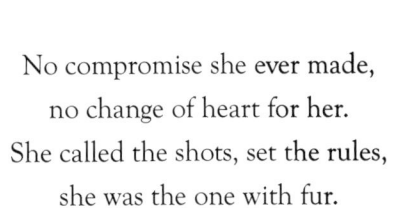

No compromise she ever made,
no change of heart for her.
She called the shots, set the rules,
she was the one with fur.

Who'd ever think a waiflike cat
could rule a family home?
That's one of life's real mysteries,
the answer still unknown.

Does anyone love us?

Ornithologists hate us
and so do gardeners too.
We're a bit like Millwall Football club,
loved by very few.
You call us wayward misfits,
the scoundrels on the block.
So please forget the boundary lines,
We'll just ignore the lot.

We'll pee in your petunias
and dig up all your seeds,
and beat up all your fluffy friends,
and shove them in the weeds.
We pride ourselves in torment
and driving dogs insane,
by sitting on the garden fence
with a look of great disdain.

Wouldn't life be empty
without us errant chaps ?
Who would keep you free of mice
and all those nasty rats?
The answer to this problem
is plain as you could see.
Welcome us for what we are
and not how we should be.

My Cat Billy

Billy loves to be outside,
especially in the mud.
We always know when he's back in
because we hear the thud.

Billy's now in trouble,
he's ripped the rug once more.
Last week he snagged the carpet,
it's now frayed by the door.

He always seems to break the rules,
he never seems to learn.
Mummy even had a shout
when Billy broke her fern.

Mummy got so angry
and threw him back out side,
but I let Billy back indoors
and Billy went to hide.

Billy cat makes a mess
when eating from his dish,
and Mummy says he's even worse
if he's been eating fish.

He's really disobedient,
he steals food all the time.
But I don't call it stealing
when the food he's got is mine!

The footprints found on Dads' new car
belong to Billy cat.
He was snoozing on the bonnet
where he was stretched out flat.

Everyone is sick and tired
of Billy's naughty ways,
but I just think he's wonderful
and hope he always stays.

My Terms

Oh yes, of course I really heard you,
your voice is like a drill.
The sound that goes right through me,
just like the winter chill.
So what is wrong in sitting
in the middle of the road?
I'll come in when I'm ready
And not because I'm told !

Yes, cars will have to wait for me,
it's written in my rules.
I decide what's best for me
and not you human fools.
What do you mean it's dangerous?
I have more lives than you.
A full eight more to be exact
and I've only used up two.

The Cats Chorus

They sat upon the old stone wall
with voices ready for the nightly call.
What's the din? That noise? That row?
Oh, it's the four old boys on their nightly prowl.

You may consider it's a dreadful sound.
To their eight ears it's 'sense around'!
Old Mitch is known as the tenor voice,
the deep low bass supplied by Boyce.

The two descanters are Jet and Sid,
Percussion comes from a dustbin lid.
Across the airwaves, their songs are heard.
Ignore the protests, they're not deterred.

All the songs they sing are for their queens.
The airwaves filled with their loud screams.
Whilst they serenade and sing with flare,
they dodge the missiles without a care.

Missing You

We miss our little furry friend,
our little pussy cat.
We miss her little purring voice,
our lives are rather flat.
The fire still roars and the chair is there,
her favourite place to sleep.
In our hearts she'll always be,
a memory we will keep.

What you sacrifice by having a cat

Never own a Chesterfield,
or carpets from Japan.
Forget the look of handmade silk,
or cashmere from Milan.

Bone china is a no-go,
antiques they're now taboo.
Ideas of owning Darlington glass
would be preposterous, too.

Disregard the finest lace
from Alencon in France.
LLadro from the Doulton house,
not even sideways glance.

Objets d'art may sound quite nice,
to own them would be daft.
Including all those little things
made by children in their craft.

Dinner parties are not advised,
unless eaten in the dark.
Just take a rug for sandwiches
and consume them in the park.

The thought of lovely canapés
with all that added hair
would be too much for Gordon R,
a moment of despair.

There are many joys of having cats
too numerous to speak.
Your house will be your castle
but never the home, très chic..

The Art of Sleeping

What is wrong with sleeping?
I only take a nap.
Why venture out in the cold,
to forsake a nice warm lap?

It clearly is a science fact
that cats need forty winks.
And a further forty is just right,
another fact, me thinks.

To sleep upon those fluffy towels
is heaven sent to me.
The airing cupboard is the tops,
the greatest place to be.

Don't condemn a puss for snoozing,
just celebrate the fact.
There's nothing more worth seeing,
than a contented sleeping cat.

Growing Old Disgracefully

I'm growing old disgracefully,
it's caution to the wind.
For all my deeds will now be bad,
with nothing to rescind.

I'll climb up on the counters
and steal what's out for tea.
Then walk across the butter dish
to have a licking spree.

Nothing will be safe now,
not even cherished plates.
I'll send them for a burton
on my rampaging spates.

Whilst ascending up the kitchen blinds,
I'll swing across the floor.
All you'll see is a fuzzy shape
as I hurtle out the door.

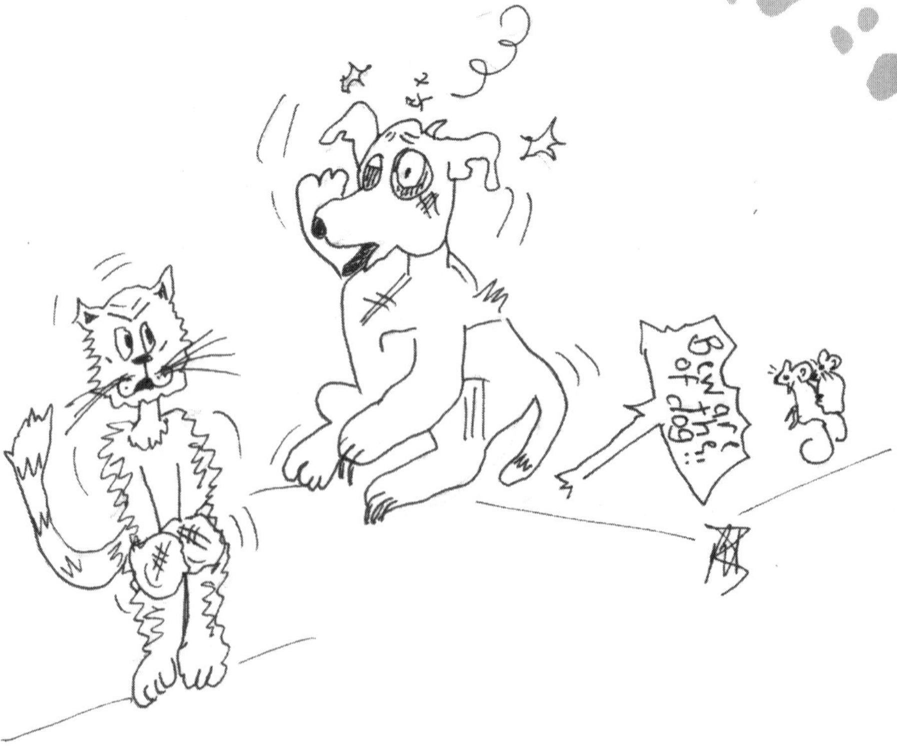
Beware of the dog...

Dog verses cats

Dogs are known as man's best friend,
with a cat that's not the case.
Canines need a walk each day,
felines need their space.

Dogs just slobber down their food,
but cats will pick and choose.
Man's best friend may pick a fight
with a cat, he's bound to lose.

Cats are really more aloof,
dogs they need a friend.
Felines may just come and go,
on dogs you can depend.

Cats will never compromise,
there is no humble pie.
But dogs, they always want to please
until the day they die.

Chillie the 'Asbo' Cat

He would be in detention
if human was his breed.
He'd have a clutch of 'Asbo's'
for every major deed.

I'm not suggesting waywardness
but neither is he good.
In fact he is a hooligan
just a baddy in 'da hood'!!

He looks just like an angel,
a feline 'Angelo'.
He has the looks of Leo,
it's only there for show.

He struts around the neighbourhood
as though it were his right,
bashing up the local cats
and giving dogs a fright.

What will become of Chillie,
who everyone adores?
Will he end up doing porridge,
with handcuffs on his paws?

Or will he turn a brand new leaf,
a paragon of peace?
Not seen on wanted posters,
the enemy of police.

There is no proper answer
to this conundrum clear.
Chillie is our special cat,
for that we love him dear.

Ladies of a Certain Age

(Dedicated to Lorraine and BoBo)

We are ladies of a certain age,
just wanting peace and calm.
We don't want ruffians, or hooligans,
they lack finesse and charm.

Scallywags and beastly brutes
stay away from us we urge.
Posh and rough just do not mix,
we're not prepared to merge.

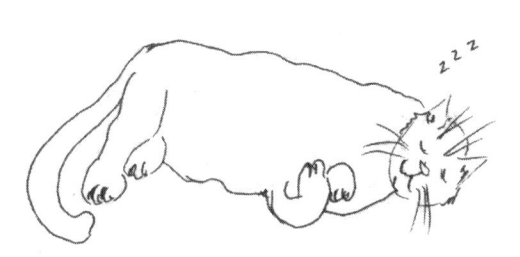

We are the belles of advancing years,
with little regard for chaps.
Our cat flap is quite sacrosanct
so leave us to our naps.

Our time is now for pampering
and stretching on fine silk.
Not running away from thuggish fiends,
or creatures of that ilk.

Gone are our desires
and temptations of the flesh.
We prefer things more exotic
like cream that's really fresh.

Party Time

I see you've got some wine again
in your human paw.
It does appear to be nearly full
just like the one before.
You say it is a Chardonnay
and you've only had a few.
I'd say its several bottles now,
and you've had eleventy-two.

Oh no, it's Karaoke time,
your friends are cheering loud.
So now we'll have 'New York, New York',
sung by a drunken crowd.
You always sing 'I will survive',
but it's me that really has.
Every year we hear this din,
when I prefer Trad Jazz.

Did I see you wobble
towards the fridge once more?
I just hope that you've now realised
it's a quarter after four.
So when you tumble into bed
at some ridiculous hour,
it's me that will take full control,
I'll be the one with power.

First of all I'll climb the blinds,
and crash them to the floor.
Followed by a wailing cry
and scratching at the door.
Finally, I'll drop a mouse
upon your snoring face.
So next time you think its party time
you'll find another place.

Bed Changing

Of course I'm very angry,
in fact I'm hoping mad.
You woke me from my slumbers
for which I'm not too glad.

There I was quite comfy,
lying on the bed,
until you yanked the duvet off
and I landed on my head.

Indeed I was just napping,
the thing that cats do best.
Now all the bedding's on the floor,
a sight I quite detest.

I face a real dilemma,
a catastrophic jam.
No one really seems to care
about just how I am.

My bedding has gone missing
and the mattress is quite bare.
I think I'll find another place
as this just isn't fair.

Holiday

I see you're going away again,
I've spotted your tartan case.
So if you expect a warm return,
you won't get any grace.

How dare you leave me on my own
with neighbours dropping in.
Lumbered with impromptu meals
and cat food from a tin.

You bet your life I'll lay the guilt
and make you feel the pain.
You'll wonder why you ever went
on holiday to Spain.

I think I'll wait a week or so
before we're friends again.
So next time you plan a trip away,
I suggest you just remain.

The Protest

I wish to make a protest,
I want to state my case.
She's gone and bought me cheaper food,
it's a national disgrace.

She says she's making economies,
and tightening her belt,
so my potions are of meagre size
and now I'm looking svelte.

Surely there's a Minister
for us disgruntled cats,
to represent our woeful plight
and sort out all our spats.

The national court of feline rights
should clearly be involved,
to stop this awful travesty
and get this matter solved.

I want this fact reported
as headlines in the news,
tell the nation of this deed,
recount this kitties views.

The queen should be alerted,
she should intervene,
to reinstate my favourite food
or return the guillotine.

Snow

You really don't expect me
to go out in all that snow.
I'm a feline with four delicate paws,
not a skater in a show.

This white stuff is too cold, you know,
it doesn't suit us cats.
Instead we like a huge log fire
and nice warm empty laps.

It's alright for you humans,
your toilet's nice and snug.
All I get is an ice cold 'toosh',
enough to freeze my blood.

I'll settle for observing you
from the window sill inside.
Watch you wobble down the path
as you slip and slide.

Wake me up at tea time
or when it's warm once more.
Just not when it's snowing white stuff
and certainly minus four.

House Rules

(Cat Style)

My meals should be both regular
and always served on time.
Excuses are forbidden,
such lateness is a crime.

No skimping on my dining time
as quality is key.
I'll throw up on your Wilton,
for that I guarantee.

Grooming is restricted,
as to when I'll let you know.
Ignore that rule at your own risk,
as displeasure I will show.

My bed should be both warm and soft.
Such comfort I expect.
Stone cold sheets just will not do,
for that I would object.

Your lap must be available for me
to rest upon each night.
A fleecy wrap or sheepskin rug
would add to my delight.

By following these golden rules,
I will remain your friend.
If straying from contractual terms,
all ceasefire will just end.

The Hunting Dilemma

The birds won't let me catch them,
despite how hard I try.
They chirp and screech around me,
mobbing as they fly.

The blackbirds are just pesky,
they complain if I go near.
I wouldn't touch those magpies, though,
they're vicious, so I hear.

What really isn't helping
is this silly little bell.
I jingle like a fairy
and sound like Tinkerbell.

I've climbed the knotted oak tree
to catch them unaware.
But squirrels launched off missiles,
there's acorns everywhere.

This hunting lark's exhausting,
and dangerous as well.
My stalking days are numbered,
how long I couldn't tell.

Boxes

I just love to sit in boxes,
any kind will do.
The bigger ones are wonderful,
but little ones are too.
I never will discriminate
in brand, or make, or name.
I'll squeeze myself inside each one,
I treat them all the same.

The posh ones are more padded,
so comfort is assured.
Little ones offer challenges,
which mustn't be ignored.
To resist a box and not squeeze in,
is hopeless for a cat.
Temptations of a cardboard box
are much to great for that.

So next time you get a hamper
from a famous London store,
or even a box from Postie
left by the pantry door,
don't throw it in the rubbish bin,
or chuck it on the fire.
Leave it for your local cats,
of it they will not tire.

Puss in Boots

(Charles Perrault was only human.)

If you're looking for perfection
you needn't look too far.
I'm the legendary Puss in Boots
and really set the bar.

I'm a charismatic character
with elegance to boot.
On many a stage I have performed,
a silver studded brute.

My presence is exceptional,
my talents are renowned.
Applause for me is rapturous,
my audience spellbound.

Red Riding Hood is tedious
and Goldilocks, a bore.
With me it's quite a different thing,
for everyone wants more.

I'm sensational in Hollywood,
as Oscar would agree.
Forget lasagne eating cats,
as now it's only me.

Humility is for all those fools
who lack my charm and wit.
I'll settle for the razzamatazz
and remain a mega hit.

So when I take my final purr
and ascend to kitty bliss,
the world will lose a superstar
and Puss in Boots you'll miss.

Therapy

Our cat, he needs some therapy
as he's petrified of mice.
He runs away from collared doves
and shakes if he sees lice.

Even in the evening,
he's frightened of the dark.
He jumps inside a cupboard
when he hears a distant bark.

If he sees his own reflection,
he hisses and he spits.
That's followed by a ten foot leap,
resulting in the splits.

We've even tried to hypnotise
our neurotic little mog.
We've played him every self help tape
and even kept a log.

He'll never be a brave cat,
or a creature of the night.
Just not to jump at shadows,
that would be alright.

Felix

(To Val, Rob and, of course, Felix)

Felix Sale R I P

If you see a tuxedo cat,
his name is Felix Sale.
Yes of course, he's black and white
complete with bushy tail.
He sees himself a local chap,
a famous leading light.
The local queens just swoon and sway,
at this perfect 'moggy' sight.

He struts around the neighbourhood
from garden fence to post,
As he weaves through all the gardens
like a silent feline ghost.
Etiquette and bylaws
are really not for him.
His approach to life is simple,
just follow every whim.

Felix would describe himself
as something rather rare.
Forget the silly pedigree,
for that he wouldn't care.
His people are frustrated
by his lack of social grace.
After washing clean his underneath,
he wants to lick their face.

Talk to the Paw

Now let's just get this thing quite clear,
is what I want to say.
Just because you can't meow,
it's not my fault, o k?

The fact you talk such gibberish,
that only humans know,
whilst I can chat in all cat speak,
dog and buffalo.

Here's a piece of advice for you,
for when you talk to me,
just cut out all the silly words
and noises like a bee.

So if you ever wonder why
I look at you so stern,
just remember the advice I give,
a lesson you should learn.

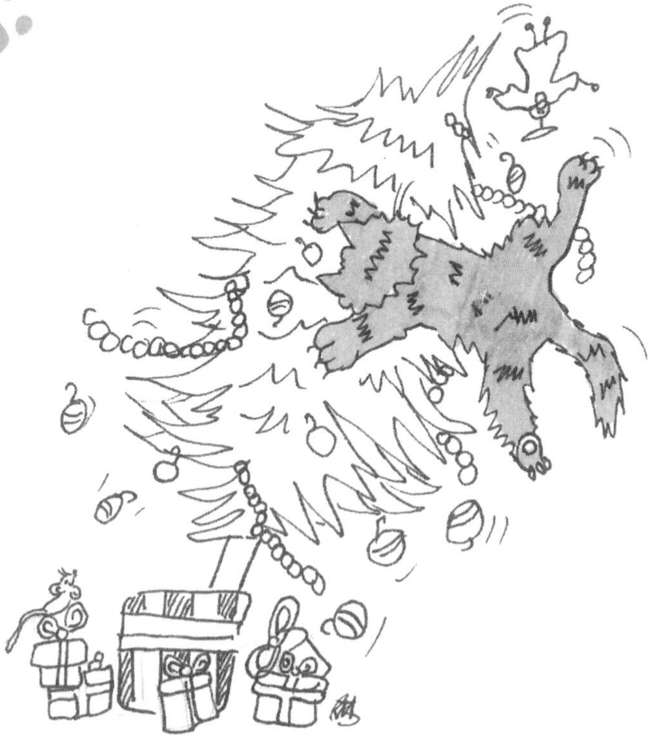

It's Christmas Time

I love it when it's Christmas,
especially the tree.
With all those lovely shiny balls
just hanging there for me.

With a nudge I'll make them move
or even knock them off.
Then chase them hard around the room,
unless I find a moth.

And then I'll climb the Christmas tree
to the fairy on the top.
I'll tug her from her nice safe spot
and watch her gently drop.

Oh dear! The tree is on the list
and now I'm falling down.
The fairy's lost her magic wand,
it's broken on the ground.

The lights are now around my neck,
still flashing off and on.
I'd better make myself quite scarce
before they see what's wrong.

Wrapping paper is my real delight,
it's the thing I love to tear.
Perhaps I'll just resist the urge
and settle on the chair.

Pottery

(with due deference to Pam Ayres!)

Who said that cats were graceful?
Who claimed that they were deft?
They've broken all me nik naks,
I now have nothing left.

I used to own Royal Dalton
and many things by Spode.
The cats have totally wrecked the lot,
they've cleared out my abode.

At least there's no more dusting
and me window sills are clear.
I'm now collecting cobwebs,
and me moneys gone on beer!

Crunchie

Have you seen our Crunchie?
He's black and white and splodgey.
His teeth are all now missing
and his right eye's really dodgy.

He doesn't wear a collar
as he's always climbing fences.
The neighbours try to stop him
but he breaks through their defences.

I suspect he's sleeping somewhere
in your garage or your shed.
But knowing Crunchie's favourite,
it's on your feather bed.

So if you find my moggie,
just point him to the door.
You'd know it if you found him,
of that I'm really sure.

Muddy Footprints

Our kitchen floor is filthy,
there's paw prints everywhere.
Old Tom has wandered back inside,
without a thought or care.

Tom's paws are really muddy,
in fact they look quite rank.
He's rolled in every puddle,
just like a furry tank.

We wouldn't be so bothered
if Tom had fewer feet.
Or stayed outside for longer
and dried them in the street.

But if Tom had been a centipede
things would be more bleak.
Imagine all those footprints
to clean would take a week.

Our Beautiful Cat

Twinkle twinkle little cat,
how cute you look upon the mat.
Your eyes are shining clear and bright,
this gives you perfect visual sight.
You sweet feline we love you so
please never leave this status quo.

Claude

Claude looked most disgruntled
when someone called him fat.
He said he had heavy frame,
befitting for a cat.

His owner called him fussy,
as he only eats best fish.
To make such matters even worse,
it's from a silver dish.

The local vet suggested
a diet of meagre size.
Claude disputed that idea
through all his protest cries.

His argument is simple,
a model he is not.
Forget the super slender,
give cream with extra shot.

Claude really wasn't happy
about the changed cuisine.
Missing was the firm rib steak
from bonny Aberdeen.

He blamed it all on Delia
and Jamie to name but two.
No more the horn of plenty,
it's the plate of very few.

The morale to Claude's story
is never trust a chef.
They influence the people,
which leaves poor Claude bereft.

His diet is now deficient,
for all the goodies gone.
His little bowl is empty,
the days now seem too long.

The Warning

I've twitched my tail to warn you off
but still you will persist.
Just leave me be and give me peace,
just listen to my hiss.

You've pushed your luck,
it's time to pay, my claws are ready now.
I'm swiping at your flabby flesh,
until I make you yowl.

Perhaps next time you'll think again
and leave me to my snooze.
Or I will have to scratch your arm
and cause that bloody ooze.

Cat on a hot tin roof

It's not that I'm complaining,
it's not that I'm perturbed.
I can not lie on this shed roof,
my sleep is now disturbed.

Why did you change the fabric
from felt to rotten tin?
I cannot walk upon that roof
to get my napping in.

My paws are rather delicate
for such intensive heat.
So please remove this hot tin roof,
just consider my poor feet.

I like a little sunny spot
to rest my weary head,
but this tin roof is like kiln
or an oven for fresh bread.

The option is quite obvious,
you need to ditch the roof.
My little paws are smouldering,
just look, I have the proof!

Number Ten

Oh, I see you need to use me
as a servant of the realm.
To chase the vermin from your house,
those rats that overwhelm.

The press have now reported
that you're overrun by rats.
They scurry under bushes
and stroll across your mats.

My fee is by the hour
with a bonus at the end.
If it's good enough for bankers
I'll follow in that trend.

If Humphrey hadn't been kicked out,
and retired from catching mice,
you wouldn't have those nasty rats
and life would be just nice.

(Humprey the cat from number 10 Downing St was pensioned off and not replaced, until rats were spotted. The new appointee, Larry, was unavailable for comment, but probably would have said the above !)

10

Marlene's Cat

Marlene's cat is Mabel,
such a feisty little queen.
Her temperament is tetchy,
just cranky and quite mean.

To contemplate a cuddle
would be a big mistake.
The very thought of those sharp claws
is a chance you shouldn't take

Mabel is so beautiful,
her fur so soft and lush.
A disposition that is strange,
'cause she's never had a brush!

Marlene tried to groom her once,
the scars confirm that fact.
Mabel had a hissing fit
and that put paid to that.

It's truly quite astounding
how the M's can co-exist.
They rub along together
in strange domestic bliss.

Marlene's solved the problem,
she now gives Mabel loves.
She's purchased the solution,
she wears asbestos gloves.

Delicious

I see you're having dinner,
a gourmet meal I'd say.
I'll sit and watch you eat it,
just like every day.

That fish looks quite delicious
just laying on your plate.
You know I'll always help you,
I'll hang around and wait.

You wolfed down all the fish then,
excluding bone and skin.
I see you have a pudding,
a sickly creamy thing.

You need to be more careful,
your load will widen more.
Those hips will be enormous,
with that belly on the floor.

I'm thinking of your waistline,
your health is my concern.
So relinquish all those goodies
and let me take your turn.

The answer is quite simple,
I'll have to eat your food.
I see you're not impressed then,
but you needn't be so rude!

New Comer

I'm feeling quite depressed today,
I'm feeling rather flat.
My people have done the dirty
and got another cat.
This deed is quite preposterous,
a felony, I'd say.
Consider what's been done to me
and take this foe away.

I will not share my sleeping place
or favourite garden spot.
Forget the chance of buddies, mate,
as your demise I'll plot.
I'll hiss and spit and growl a lot,
my feelings will be known.
Objections will be vocal
and my disapproval shown.

Forget a truce or amnesty,
you haven't got a chance.
Just pack away and clutter off
without a backward glance.
The cat flap will be opened
for you to take your leave.
I'll assist your quick departure
with a massive shove and heave.

Adoptee

I see that I'm not wanted
by the way you hiss and spit.
You swipe me if I get too near,
my wounds still sting a bit.

Our people claim you're friendly,
but I would disagree.
You spend you time just swearing
and it's mainly aimed at me.

You guard the kitchen doorway
like a soldier on parade.
I'd love to come and have a snack,
but I'm really quite afraid.

You shove me out the cat flap
to confront the cold night air.
Then you barricade the entrance
which I feel is most unfair.

Is there room for arbitration,
or will this war go on?
Or should I take up 'kitsu',
to make me big and strong?

I just want you to be friendly,
a buddy, and my mate.
Maybe I'll find a new abode
to be a surrogate.

Feisty Feline

(Dedicated to those like Lorraine
who have introduced a new comer to their home)

Will you stop that awful hiss
and put away your claw !
That snarling sound is dreadful
but I've told you that before.

You don't look so attractive
with fur stood up on end.
Why can't you be a nice cat
to this little feline friend?

Look! I know it is your food bowl
but you needn't stand on guard.
You're being rather silly,
thinking kittens can be barred.

Growling isn't fetching
for Persian such as you.
I thought you were a lady,
I think that's gone askew.

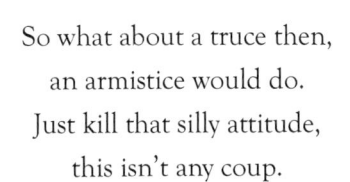

So what about a truce then,
an armistice would do.
Just kill that silly attitude,
this isn't any coup.

Sulking isn't clever,
and it will not change the fact,
that we have a new arrival
so just get over that!

Your cat or me?

I'll go and pack your bag then.
You've made your feelings clear.
You told me that my cat must go.
Alas it's you, I fear.

You said my cat was ugly
as he gave you evil looks.
I think its called perception,
he's handsome in my books.

You never really liked him,
and wouldn't pet his fur.
You said I loved him more than you,
with that I would concur.

We could have been a family,
all homely and in love.
Instead you called my cat grotesque,
so it's you I have to shove.

You needn't bother bleating
or telling me I'm hard.
Just close the door on your way out,
and the key you can discard.

The moral of this story
is never make me choose.
My cat is here forever
and he will never lose.

Sisters 1
(Branston's Story)

My sister has just cuffed me
and revenge is on my mind.
I'll pounce on her much later,
I'll attack her from behind.

She claims she is much smarter
and pushes me around.
I always get her back though
when I pin her to the ground.

She thinks she's really pretty
as her fur is almost grey.
But I'm the one who's sociable
and really likes to play.

My sister is quite sneaky,
she always gets the bed.
She growls when I go near it
and swipes me round the head.

I always win the war though
because I always wait.
Whilst she's dreaming of those birds,
I hoover up her plate!

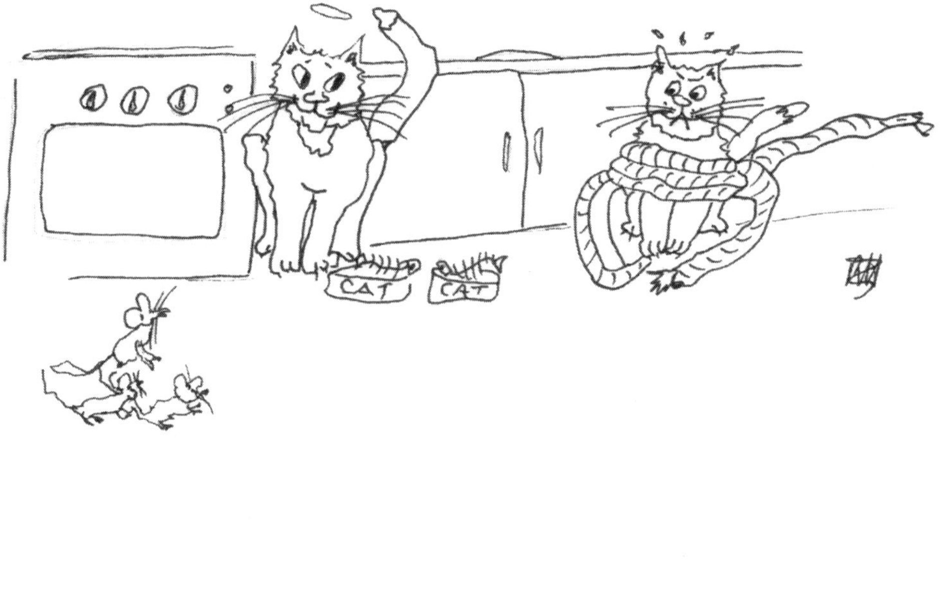
CAT
CAT

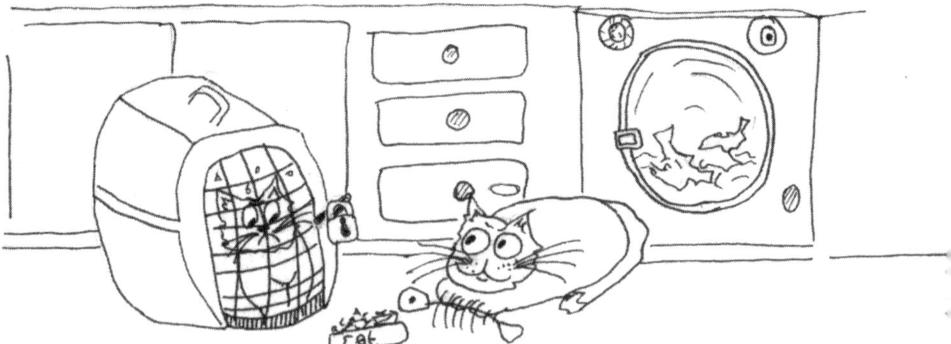

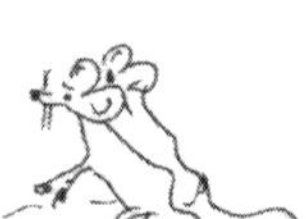

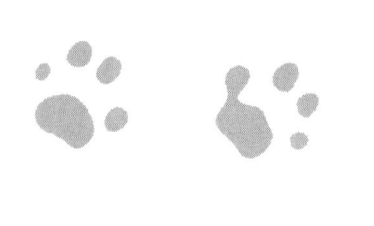

Sisters 2
(Smog's Story)

I cuffed my little sister
as she ate my bowl of food.
Her manners are disgusting,
she's sneaky and most rude.

My skill for hunting mice and birds,
stupendous I would say.
She of course would argue
I'd seen a better day!!

She thinks that she is so clever,
and has the upper paw,
but when I clout her on the stairs
I leave her nose quite sore.

She tries to share my feather bed
and I warn her with a growl.
Our people think she's rather cute,
but goodness knows just how?

I have a cunning plan in mind
to ambush her tonight.
I'll wait until she's fast asleep
before I start the fight.

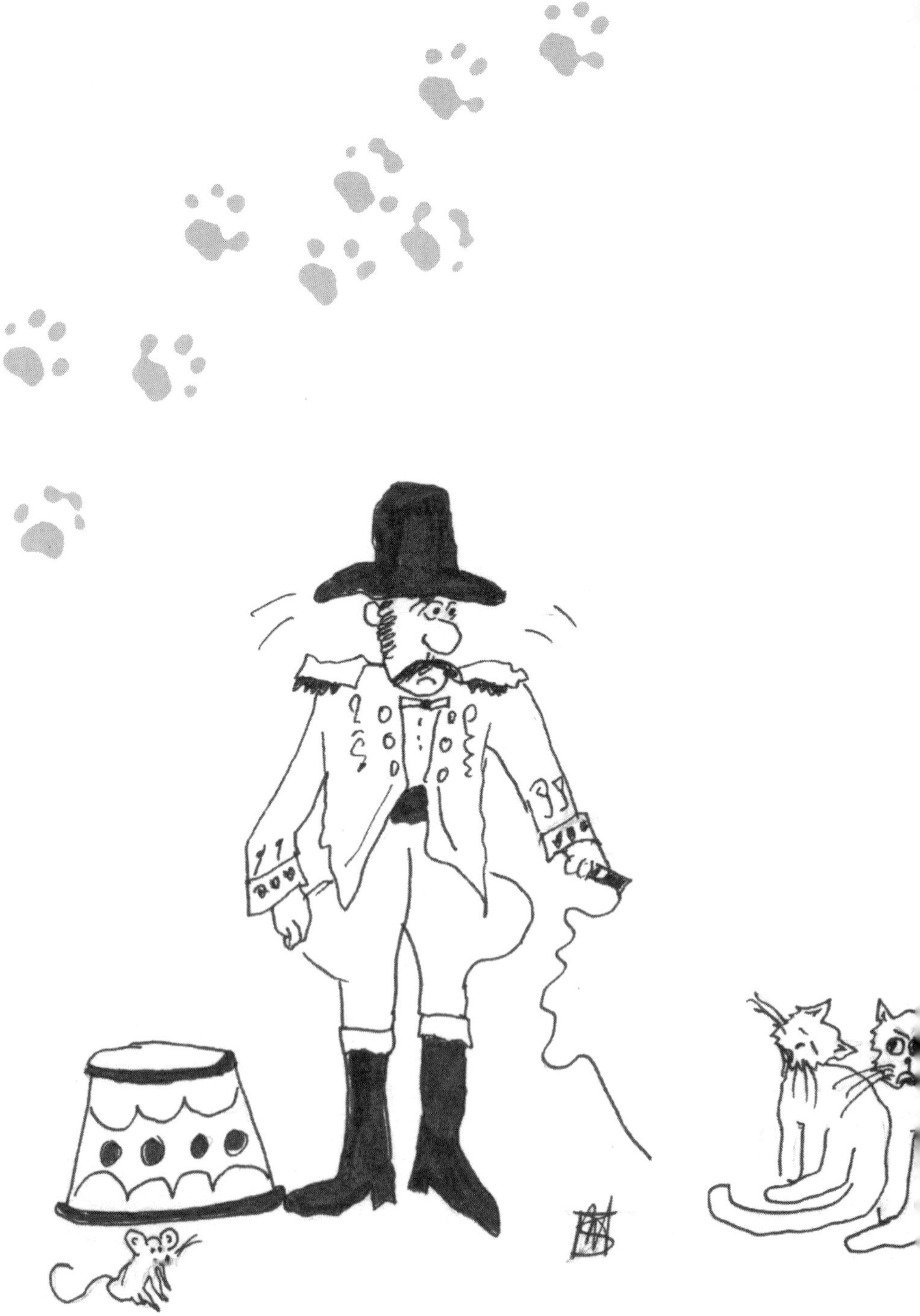

Training

The plan was to include some
in a circus taming act.
Instead the felines showed them
don't try to train a cat.

No matter how they tempted them
the cats remained nonplussed.
Instead they yawned and went to sleep
as they couldn't see the fuss.

An ambitious trainer came along
to teach them how to dance.
The cats just looked him up and down,
he didn't stand a chance.

The cats just sat there grooming
as he struggled on his own.
They treated him with cold contempt,
aloofness he was shown.

The moral of this story is
you cannot train a cat.
They're smarter than the average man
and that remains a fact.

Pond Skater

I thought the ice was thicker,
It should have held my weight.
I now look like a scrawny rat,
my fur's in such a state.

The blanket weed is horrid,
it's hanging off my coat.
I look just like a slimy fiend
from an island quite remote.

Those goldfish were inviting,
I thought I'd take a peep.
I didn't know I'd take a dive
in water that was deep.

You may find this saga funny
to see this cat who's wet.
But it will cost quite dearly
if I need to see a vet.

So rather than just laughing
perhaps you'll fetch a towel.
Whilst I just stand here dripping
and smelling rather foul.

All Shapes and Sizes

I'm a cat of a certain stature,
there are those who'd call me stout.
Inside this sagging carcass
is a tiger bursting out.
You may find this thought outlandish,
and even quite bizarre.
But laugh out loud hysterically?
It's one step just too far.

So my waistline has expanded,
its circumference is great.
Just cut out all your carping,
you're making me irate.
You'll find I'm like a panther,
just waiting there to pounce.
What do you mean by saying
I look as though I'd bounce?

Perhaps I'm not so sylphlike,
or that vision from the wild.
But calling me the cubby chops
is getting me more riled.
There's a cheetah deep inside me,
with turbo boost for speed.
So never underestimate
this ferocious beast indeed.

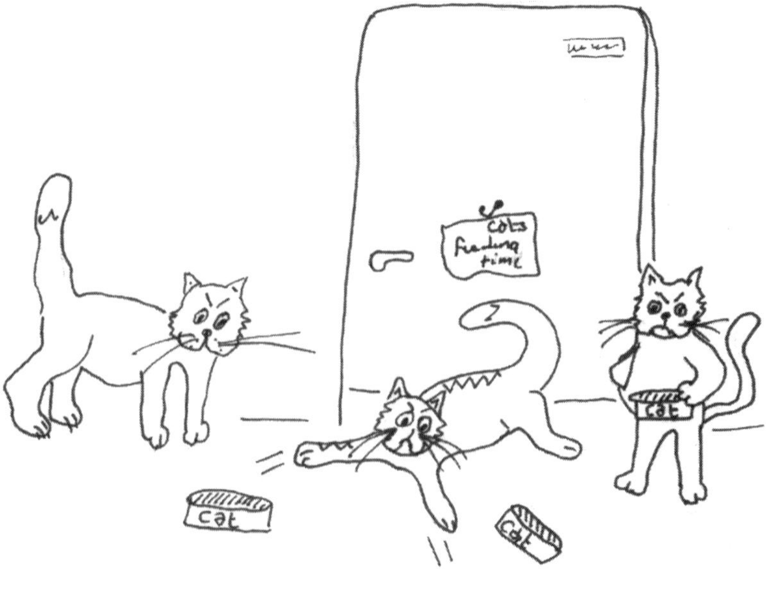
Cats
feeding
time
cat
cat
cat

Hunger Pangs

Is it time for breakfast, Mum?
We'd really like to know.
Supper was three hours ago,
there's a rumbling down below.

Our stomachs are now yowling
for a morsel, or a snack.
So a nice, big, juicy chicken leg
would put an end to that.

We've now become delirious,
through hunger we are sure.
Its been three hours since we were fed,
no more can we endure !

So let us have a nice plump steak,
or salmon on a plate.
For that would end our hunger pangs,
at least till half past eight.

Ted

I want to tell you a story
about a cat called Ted.
He's certainly a legend,
although he's far from dead.

Ted, he is a scallywag
and a loveable rogue to boot.
But he hasn't any scruples,
as your kitchen he will loot.

Your Sunday roast will be fair game,
as Ted will help himself.
So never think the meat is safe,
because it's on a shelf.

Your sausages will vanish,
from your work top or a ledge.
You'll probably see your chicken leg
go vanish through the hedge.

Lamb and pork are favourites
of this little feline thief.
Across the lawn he will run,
with a chop between his teeth.

Ted just looks and sniffs the air,
as if he rules the patch.
No doubt he's hatched a cunning plan
which humans can not match.

Neighbours they do curse him
and try and to block his way.
But Ted's a slippery customer
and always wins the day.

One day when Ted has gone
to that cattery in the sky,
you'll see this eerie feline form
and a paw print in your pie.

Flea Spray

Don't you bring that spray near me,
or I'll leg it out the door.
I'm not the host of nasty fleas,
so your argument is poor.

What evidence do you have, I ask?
Was it when I scratched?
Do you think I wouldn't know
if some foul things were hatched?

Please spend your time more earnestly
by seeing to my needs.
Instead of entomology
and the lifecycle of fleas.

Bafflement

There is this thing that's worrying me,
a conundrum as it stands.
I'm baffled how they manage
getting Friesians in those cans.

I've never seen a single cat
stalking any herds.
It's only ever mice and rats
or unsuspecting birds.

It's difficult to comprehend
how a cat could catch a bull.
Something weighing several tons
would take a lot of pull.

Just to add another twist,
that's how do cats catch sheep?
Do they stalk them late at night,
When they are fast asleep?

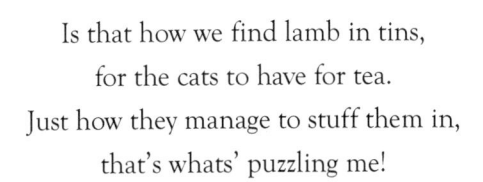

Is that how we find lamb in tins,
for the cats to have for tea.
Just how they manage to stuff them in,
that's whats' puzzling me!

I would say the perfect meal
would be a can of rat.
Or mouse in gravy would be nice,
So what is wrong with that?

The Eyes of Scratch Springet
(R.I.P March 2012)

There is something quite beguiling
about a feline's eyes.
They kind of mesmerise you,
with that look that's very wise.

Our Scratch, she's no exception,
her eyes see everywhere.
She notes each little nuance
from curled up in her chair.

Her amber eyes invite you
to stroke her silken coat.
But never misinterpret
as anger she'll denote.

She may be rather aged now,
but don't be fooled by that.
Her eighteen years have taught her,
to be a savvy cat.

Her name may mystify you,
as Springet is quite strange.
If I tried to explicate it,
you'd think me most deranged.

So, back to Scratch's eyes then,
and the fact they see it all.
From mice right down garden,
to the birds just on the wall.

You see those eyes just watching
every move or step you take.
If there's any hint of food stuff,
she's there just like a shake.

So despite her fragile body,
and her gait that now is slow,
her amber eyes still twinkle
as she is in the know!

Broken Flowers

That crazy cat from number three
has broken all me flowers.
He's squashed the lot, he's lost the plot,
me blooms that took me hours.

I saw him pounce, I saw him charge,
across me flower bed.
He's really nuts, a crazy klutz,
And now I'm seeing red.

A thorny bush will go there now
to stop this feline scamp.
His game is done, there's no more fun.
No more the garden champ.

Furry Pants

Never wear dark colours
or suits from Saville Row.
You'll end up like a Yeti,
abominable from the snow.

Always check your derrière,
when walking out the door,
as you'll be covered rich in fur,
a hairy 'toosh' once more.

It's wise to warn your dinner guests,
before they dine with you,
or they will sprout a shaggy coat
like something from the zoo.

Cats do not discriminate
in what you choose to wear.
They'll settle for just anything
to remove unwanted hair.

Cashmere, wool or mohair
they couldn't give a fig.
You'll still resemble someone
that wears a furry wig.

So listen to this warning,
take heed in what I say,
ignore this at your peril
or you will rue the day.

Archie, the Wonder Cat

Archie's just like Beckham,
he can really bend a ball.
He's even good with bits of foil
he'll thwack 'em at the wall.

The way he leaps around for moths,
would make a goalie proud.
Archie's entertaining,
he can always pull a crowd.

He's faster than Usain Bolt,
when he's chasing after mice.
No doubt he's smashed the minute mile,
we think its more than twice.

Sir Ranulph Finnes is envious
of our mountaineering cat,
as he scales up into oak trees
in thirty seconds flat.

He has no need for climbing kit,
or crampons for his paws.
He bounces up just like a ball,
just gripping with his claws.

Ali is disgruntled,
as Archie will not fight.
When other cats attack him
he runs away in fright.

Archie's not an aqua cat,
and hates it when its wet.
Even Michael Phelps himself
cannot tempt him yet.

Apart from fights and swimming,
Archie gets the gold.
Unless he is away that day
with a nasty feline cold.

That's not funny

So why are you just laughing,
as I'm stuck up in this tree?
You should have phone the fire brigade
to come and rescue me.

Is it that hysterical
to see a cat in need?
A poor defenceless little soul,
who needs a friend indeed.

So what if it's only twenty feet,
it's nearly out in space.
There should be an urgent rescue plan
to save my skin, post haste!

I'm so glad you find it funny,
so amusing and a farce.
Just wait until my feet touch ground
and I'm standing on the grass.

Cat Protection will be hearing
about my perilous plight.
I'll tell them that you're cruel and mean
and they'll punish you with might.

You will regret not calling
at least the National Guard.
The solution was so simple
but instead you made it hard.

Next time you see a kitty
stuck up in a tree,
you will resist that snigger
and urge to laugh with glee.

Make sure you use the speed dial
for emergency support,
to save that poor unfortunate puss
from having to contort.

The Bruiser

We've got this big old bruiser cat,
he's always having fights.
He never seems to lose them though,
despite the many bites.

We tried to keep him locked indoors,
away from all the strife.
He howls and grizzles and mews like mad,
just like some old fish wife.

Our neighbours have complained to us
about our Jack the Lad.
They think he is delinquent
but we know he's not that bad.

We've tried to curb his appetite
for punch ups and affray.
It would take a super-soaker,
or a miracle, I would say.

He never seems to toe the line,
he couldn't give a hoot.
Any disturbance on block,
it's always our old brute.

When asleep he looks divine,
an innocent little face.
It's really in those waking hours
that he's a real disgrace.

We think he's got a good side,
but we haven't found it yet.
I suppose we could wait patiently,
but I wouldn't take a bet.

Anti Cat Flap

Should I trust that nasty thing?
That contraption is insane.
I suggest that you refer to plan,
and start once more again.

I will not use that cat flap,
I insist you open doors.
The very notion of a trap,
to open with my paws.

With a pedigree that's noble
and standards that are high,
I'll really have to ask you
why you'd think I'd even try?

I want to see a doorman,
some dedicated chap,
I'd find that more preferable
than that confounded flap.

Trick of the Tail

I have this furry, swishing thing,
I'm trying hard to seize.
I've tried to chase it round and round,
instead I start to wheeze.

At times it seems quite bushy,
at least six inches thick,
and other times it's rather strange
with a tendency to flick.

I've caught it in the cat flap,
that made me want to yelp.
Folk have even trod on it,
that really didn't help.

Other cats attack it
and take out quite a bite.
I better take more care of it
and keep it out of sight.

Talking

Will you please stop talking,
this cat here needs a rest.
Your incessant, constant chatter
puts my patience to the test.

I don't want to hear about Arthur
and how his hemorrhoids hurt,
or about your cousin Sadie
and the fact that she's a flirt.

I want a chance to rest my bones
and close my weary eyes,
and drift off into happy land
with loud contented sighs.

Instead I hear you chit- chat
to your friends upon the phone,
where you talk about the weather
and your holidays in Rome.

What about my welfare,
my need to catch those zzz's ?
A little more decorum there,
and quietness, if you please.

Morris

I'm really feeling anxious
but there's worse to follow yet.
It's time to take our Morris
along to see the vet.

Oops, he's seen the cat-box,
he's running for the door.
I'll have to rugby tackle him,
to get him on the floor.

Now he's started spitting
and his claws are stuck in me.
He's howling like a banshee
with the most pathetic plea.

It's for the best , it's for his good,
I try to say to him.
He carries on resisting me
and things are looking grim.

Morris has escaped now,
he's charged his way outside.
He's disappeared through nextdoors hedge,
to find a place to hide.

I've been and phoned the vet just now
and told him of this tale.
We've rearranged the visit
for this feisty feline male.

Frog

Why are you quite so angry?
Why the need to shout?
I've only caught a little frog,
so what's the fuss about?

Do you want to share it?
I'm sure it tastes quite nice.
You just seem to scream a lot,
just like when I catch mice.

Now you've made me drop the frog,
it's hopped across the floor.
Oh dear, it's taken such a leap,
it's through the pantry door.

Perhaps if you stopped screaming
you'd help me catch this frog.
Or I'll have to fetch another
from that lovely muddy bog.

The Reluctant Hunter

Kitty cat can't catch a bird,
which many folk find quite absurd.
To watch the world quite undisturbed,
her time to hunt has been deferred.

Union

Felines of the world unite,
things in life just don't seem right.
Veggie food for cats is wrong.
Our moans and gripes, they could be long.

Leads and collars are for dogs
and never for discerning mogs.
Instead we need a comfy chair.
That demand, we think, is fair

Worming cats is cruel and mean,
sprays for fleas, we find obscene.
Just let us have some peace and rest.
So now it's said and off our chest!

Locked door

What's behind that closed, locked, door?
What is behind that door?
Is it all exciting stuff,
the kind you want to gnaw?

Does it squeak, or run around,
or is it in a cage?
Please, just let me take a peek,
I've waited for an age.

I hear a kind of movement,
like a something on a wheel.
A nice, big, chubby hamster,
a lovely tasty meal?

So don't be such a spoilsport
and push that door ajar.
Be more like the jolly good sort,
the one you know you are.

Partners

I love my cat and he loves me,
we are the best of friends.
We play together everyday
until the evening ends.

My cat, he even sleeps with me
upon my cosy bed.
He nuzzles up so close to me,
he's better than my Ted.

My cat and I hate thunderstorms,
so we always hide away.
We wait until the very last bang
before we start to play.

I worry when I go to school
that my cat's on his own.
I asked my mum to buy my cat
his very own mobile phone.

So when I'm in my classroom,
learning ABC,
my cat just stays inside all day
waiting there for me.

Mummy tells me not to fret
as my cat likes to sleep.
She finds him in her sewing box,
in a nice, warm, curled-up heap.

She Had To Go You Know

She truly had to go, you know,
she really couldn't stay.
The epitome of an outdoor cat,
the one who caught her prey.

Nothing would ever lure her back,
not even a roaring fire.
The wide beyond was her temptress,
it was her hearts desire.

The trappings of domestic life
were really not for her.
Instead she wanted the elements
to rustle through her fur.

Brief visits were enough for her,
with occasional scraps of food.
A little stroke and fuss was enjoyed,
if she was in the mood.

She truly had to go you know,
she really couldn't stay.
The epitome of an outdoor cat,
she might be back one day.

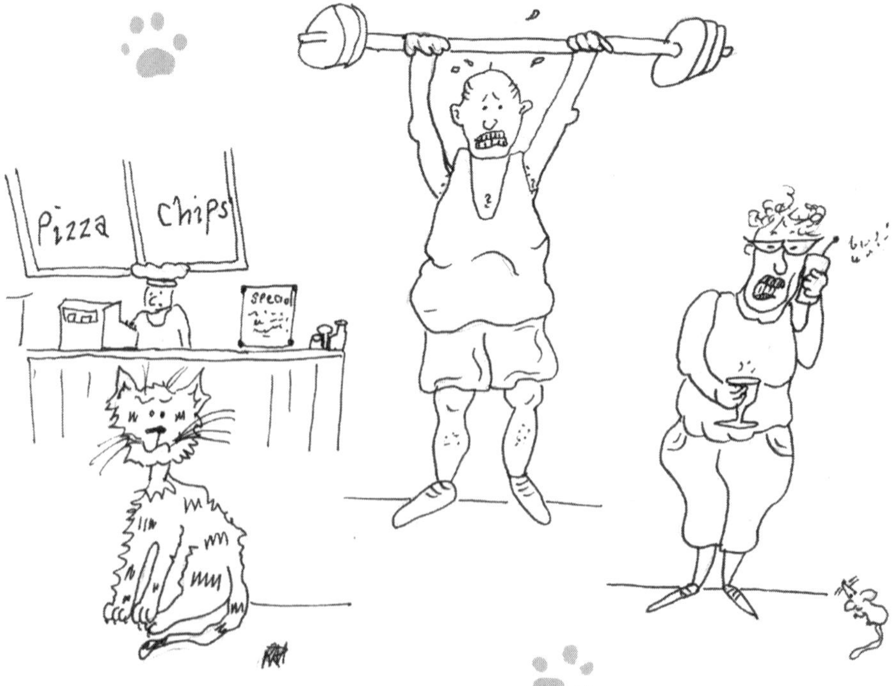
Pizza
Chips
Special

Humans

I look upon the human race
as strangely odd and out of place.
They rush around and talk on phones,
they stand in queues with all their moans.
My feline eyes observe their plight,
then I will stretch, is that alright?

These human beings are quite bizarre,
they never walk, just use the car.
Many can be found in gyms
to trim their bulks and strengthen limbs.
My feline eyes just look and learn,
I will resist and miss my turn.

They eat and drink as though half starved,
the amount consumed could be just halved.
Some chocolate cake chased down with gin
and lettuce leaf to reverse the sin.
My feline eyes just watch and note,
so smug am I, as I sit and gloat.

'Rocks'

Please let me read my paper,
just let me read the facts.
There is another world out there,
beyond the needs of cats.

What about the headlines,
the gossip and the sleaze ?
A little glance to see what's what,
two minutes if you please.

So can I do the crossword?
Or see the full time score?
Before you jump onto the page,
and shred it with your claw.

So the paper is a no-no then?
I'll fold it up instead.
Why would I read the Sunday news,
from my nice, warm, comfy bed ?

I suppose you want your breakfast?
So I better move my butt,
'cause I know you won't stop stalking me,
by the way you start to strut.

So maybe after dining,
you'll let me see the news.
Just a flick through any sports page,
To read the football views.

I'll settle down to read then,
and you can have a snooze.
But can you find another lap,
not this one that you choose.

The Week

Monday's cat is full of mouse,
replete upon the bed.
Tuesday's cat is yowling loud,
just wanting to be fed.
Wednesday's cat has nicked a koi,
from next doors well stocked pond.
Thursday's cat has missed the vet,
he decided to abscond.
Friday's cat is fast asleep,
with four paws in the air.
Saturday's cat is stalking birds,
without a single care.
Sunday's cat has dirty feet,
and trampled mud inside.
Which takes us back to Monday's cat,
and another homicide?

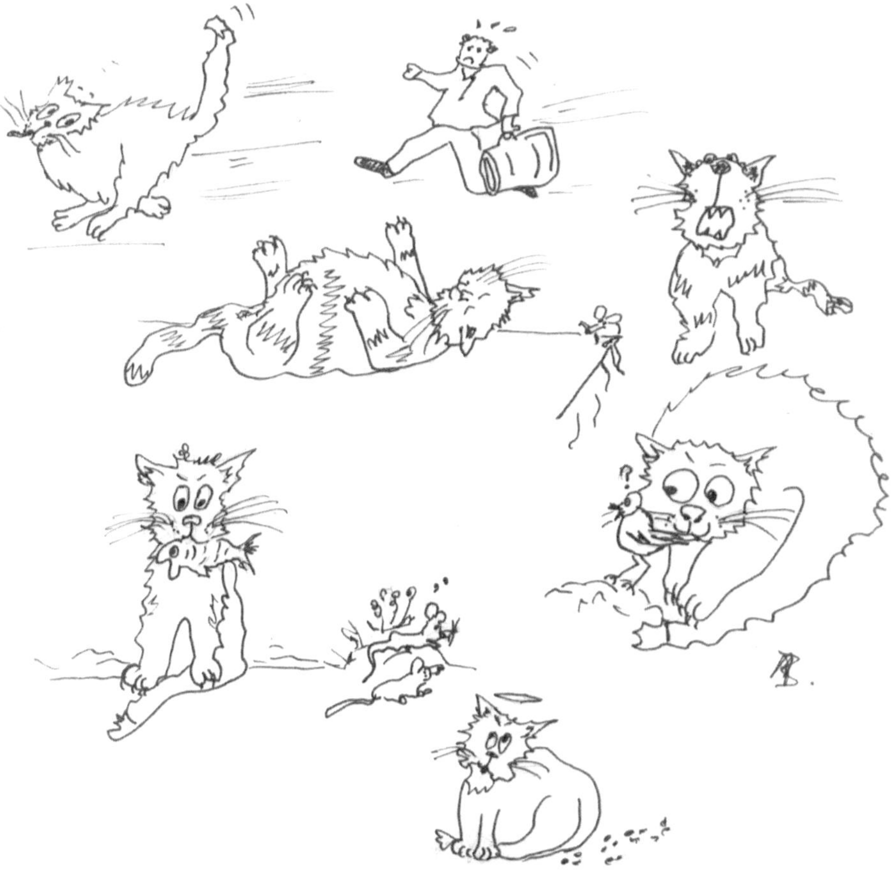

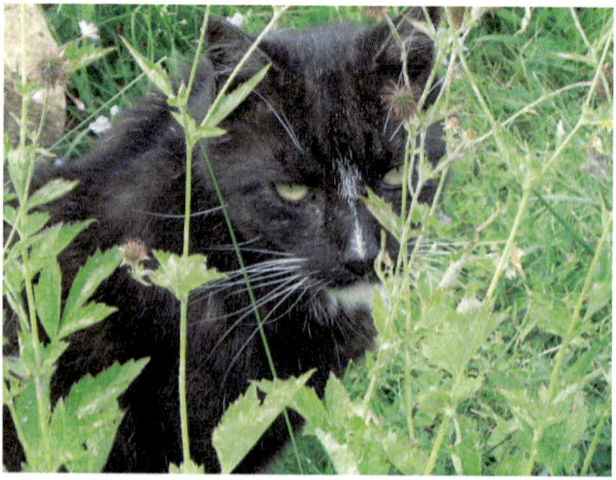

Growing Old
(Sniff, the big guy! R.I.P. September 2011)

There is nothing good about growing old,
you lose your teeth and feel the cold.
Biscuits are now hard to chew,
its not much fun when teeth are few.

That glossy coat that was so sleek,
now looks dishevelled and not so chic.
Such indignity when growing old,
as every ailment takes it's hold.

I resist all urge to chase a bird,
the very thought now seems absurd.
No kittenish ways or looking sweet,
just graying fur and less upbeat.

You haven't turned your back on me,
the real McCoy is what you see.
With my fragile frame and slowing gait,
You remain my friend, my real soul mate.

Ownership

You'll never own a cat,
it is an absolute fact.
However hard you try,
or the many tears you cry.
And that's the end of that.

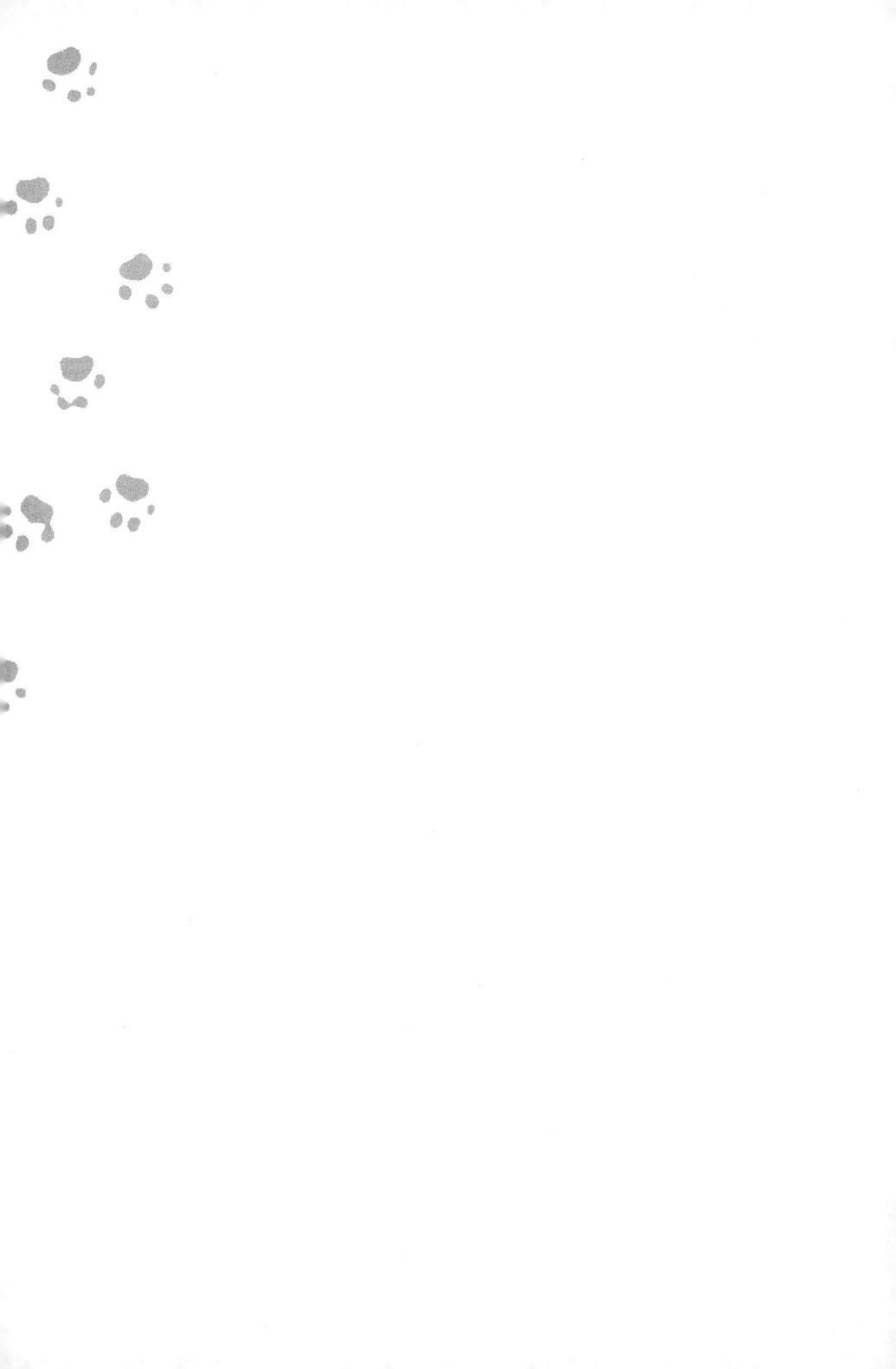